The
Team Building Strategies
of
Steve Kerr

How the NBA Head Coach of

the Golden State Warriors Creates a Winning Culture

Leadership Case Studies

Additional Leadership Case Studies

The Turnaround Strategies of Jim Harbaugh

The Motivational Techniques of Urban Meyer

The Management Ideas of Nick Saban

The Strategy Concepts of Bill Belichick

The Leadership Lessons of Gregg Popovich

The Work Ethic of Tom Brady, Peyton Manning, and Aaron Rodgers

Table of Contents

Introduction

In his first season as NBA head coach, Steve Kerr took the Golden State Warriors to an NBA Championship. In his second year as head coach, the Warriors finished the season with a record of 73-9, the best record in the history of the NBA.

At first glance, it may seem like the answer to his success is a very simple factor. He has Steph Curry on his team. When a coach is blessed with a transcendent superstar, then it may appear as if winning should be easy. Simply throw the ball out there and let your superstar win the game.

However, managing talent is not that easy. Building up a team of of professional basketball players to achieve success is never that simple. Managing egos, keeping them engaged, and allowing your players to shine are just some of the tasks that all leaders must manage in order to get their team to perform at an elite level.

In this Leadership Case Study, we analyze and highlight the ways in which Steve Kerr built a strong team culture. We focus on the concepts and ideas that helped Kerr win an NBA championship in his debut season, and led the team to win the most regular season games in history.

Part 1 covers the FOUNDATION that Kerr took before he even became a head coach. We explain how Kerr learned from great mentors and took the time and effort to prepare for his opportunity.

Part 2 discusses the actual steps that Steve Kerr took to build up his TEAM CULTURE. The Golden State Warriors have been able to achieve a high level of success in Kerr's first two seasons, and we analyze the management ideas that Steve Kerr installed when taking over the head coaching duties.

Part 3 of the case study highlights the MINDSET that Steve Kerr holds about success, and how he applies it to his team. Kerr is able to keep his players loose and interested in winning, while at the same time giving them the space and freedom to relax and enjoy the process.

The lessons that can be learned from Steve Kerr and the Golden State Warriors are not simply about basketball. Although we include a few incidences from the basketball court to highlight some key lessons, most of the management and team building ideas from this case study can be applied to any situation. Whether you are a coach, a teacher, or a business manager looking to create a better organization, the lessons of Steve Kerr can be applied to your situation.

To help you in using these lessons, there are a few review questions listed after each section to help guide you in applying them to your own business or program.

All information in this case study has been collected from public sources. Links to the full articles and other case studies are available at our website leadershipcasestudies.com.

Background Information about Steve Kerr

Date of Birth: September 27, 1965 in Beirut, Lebanon.

College Education: University of Arizona, Degree in General Studies with Emphasis in History, Sociology, and English, 1986.

NBA Playing Experience:

1988-1989: Phoenix Suns
1989-1992: Cleveland Cavaliers
1992-1993: Orlando Magic
1993-1998: Chicago Bulls
1999-2001: San Antonio Spurs
2001-2002: Portland Trail Blazers
2002-2003: San Antonio Spurs

NBA Championships Won As A Player:
Chicago Bulls: 1996, 1997, 1998
San Antonio Spurs: 1999, 2003

Playing Awards:
1997 - NBA 3-Point Shootout Champion

Head Coaching Experience:
2015-2016: Golden State Warriors

National Championships as a head Coach:
Golden State Warriors: 2015

Head Coaching Awards:
2016: NBA Coach of the Year

Part One: Laying the Foundation

In his first year as an NBA head coach, Steve Kerr coached his team to an NBA championship. In his second year as head coach, Kerr was able to guide his team to the best regular season win total in NBA history.

Although having an transformative player like Stephen Curry will always help a coach's record, Kerr's ability to lead his team to success simply cannot be denied. He has been able to quickly achieve success at the difficult job of being an NBA coach.

How did he do this? How was Kerr able to have the knowledge, wisdom, and ability to coach a team to the championship in his very first year?

The simple fact of the matter is that Steve Kerr has been preparing for this moment for a very long time. Although it was his first year as an NBA head coach, Kerr was able to draw upon years of experience to help guide him to a championship.

Find Mentors

The first step that Kerr did was to look at his past. Throughout his playing career, Kerr was blessed with an incredible list of coaches, from whom he was able to learn and grow from. The list of coaches that Steve Kerr has played for could make up an entire wing of the basketball Hall-of-Fame.

In college, Kerr played for Lute Olson at the University of Arizona. Olson coached 24 seasons at Arizona, won 587 games and one national championship. The impact of Olsen on Kerr stayed with him as he began his new coaching career. In an interview with the New York Times, Kerr recalled his first practice with Olson, where the Arizona Wildcats were coming off a 4-24 season.

The practice was hard, lasting over three hours. "We were all in shock. But he set the tone that day, and more important, he stayed with that tone," Kerr told Andrew Keh of the New York Times. "Within two years, we were in the N.C.A.A. tournament. Within four years, we were in the Final Four."

As Keh of the NY Times writes, the great coaches that Kerr had the opportunity to learn from continued when he went to the NBA:

"Kerr spent a full season under Cotton Fitzsimmons (832 career N.B.A. victories), three and a half seasons under Lenny Wilkens (1,332), five seasons under Phil Jackson (1,155), one season under Maurice Cheeks (305), and four seasons under Gregg Popovich (971 and counting)."

While playing for these coaches, Kerr was part of 5 NBA championship winning teams.

The impact of his past coaches clearly has made an impact on Kerr and his coaching style. For example, Kerr stated that Cotton Fitzsimmons kept things light in the locker room. "He just had us laughing all the time, and that was a pretty powerful thing," Kerr recalled.

Before taking his over the Head Coach for Golden State, Kerr asked his old college coach for advice and counsel. Olson, who was 80 years old at time, told his former player to be sure he fully understood what he was getting into.

"The first thing I said was, 'Are you sure you want to go in that direction?'", Olson told Keh in his article. "In coaching, you're great as long as you win every game. But as soon as you lose, you're open for all the criticism."

When developing his offensive philosophy, Kerr was very open about his admiration of the style that Gregg Popovich was running with the Spurs. He also built upon the philosophy of Lenny Wilkins of keeping the offensive system simple, but well executed. "That's been a good lesson for me: run six or eight things really well, instead of 20 things in a mediocre fashion," Kerr said.

But the most important lesson that Kerr learned from all of his mentors was simply to be true to his ideas and principles.

"Cotton Fitzsimmons and Lenny Wilkens couldn't be more different, personality-wise," he said. "But they were both great coaches because they were themselves. And that's what all my mentors have told me: 'Just be yourself, be true to yourself, stick to your principles, and it'll work.'"

Prepare For Your Opportunity

When Steve Kerr was named the head coach of the Warriors in 2015, it was the accumulation of years of preparation. Becoming a head coach wasn't something that Steve Kerr just decided to do. Rather, it was a profession that he spent years studying while preparing himself for the right opportunity.

Back when Kerr was a player, he was already thinking ahead to a future in coaching. With great coaches such as Gregg Popovich and Phil Jackson guiding him, Kerr had ample opportunities to learn from the very best. As Lee Jenkins wrote in Sports Illustrated, Kerr kept a journal during his playing days where he wrote down his thoughts. During a recent kitchen renovation, Kerr's family came upon the journal. The journal was a treasure trove of Kerr's thoughts not just about basketball, but life in general.

"In many entries, he writes about his kids," reports Jenkins. "In some, he vents about his minutes. But in a few, he looks ahead to a future in coaching."

After Kerr retired from playing, he had the opportunity to serve as an analyst on TNT. Jenkins noted how resourceful Kerr was when he conducted interviews for the television network. Before games, Kerr and his broadcasting partner Marv Albert would interview coaches for their game prep. By having access to top NBA coaches, Kerr thought that he might as well use those opportunities to learn as much as possible. He would listen closely to the coaches and take notes at a furious pace. He would often run out of paper while taking his notes, so he would often resort to writing on the cardboard that came in his dress shirts from the dry cleaners.

Marv Albert knew that Kerr was using the opportunity to learn from current coaches, and that he was thinking ahead. "He asked some questions that might not fit on a telecast," Albert recalls, "but that he could use down the line."

Kerr used a variety of methods to study other teams and develop into the leader he is today, including visiting former coaches and teammates. When he was general manager of the Suns, he asked for – and received – an invitation to a Spurs coaching retreat during the summer of 2010 in Chicago. Having a humble attitude helped pave the way for a good relationship with former coaches. Jenkins writes, "San Antonio was overhauling its offense after being swept by the Suns. Only Kerr could pull that off, beating a team and then scoring an invite to its retreat."

In an article for Sports Illustrated, Chris Ballard noted that while Kerr planned to become a coach all along, it wasn't until he was working as a broadcaster for TNT that he really began to prepare. A year before taking over as head coach of the Warriors, he attended a sports leadership conference where he connected with former coach and TV analyst Jeff Van Gundy. Kerr had always admired Van Gundy and used this opportunity to learn the advice that he shared with would-be coaches.

Ballard writes, "Van Gundy told Kerr what he tells all aspiring coaches: **Write down everything. Everything you've learned, everything you want to do. Everything you'd change. It'll organize your thoughts. Develop your philosophy.**"

Kerr took his advice and began documenting everything in a Word file on his laptop. He noted both the major incidents to the smallest details, never knowing which things might be important to his coaching career in the future. He wrote down lessons he had learned while playing for the top coaches in college and the NBA. He also had played with some of the best players in NBA history: Mark Price, Tim Duncan, Scottie Pippen, and Michael Jordan. Again, he examined the lessons learned and included those that had made an impact. He didn't leave out anything that he might be able to use later.

To develop his coaching philosophy, he focused not only on his former teammates and coaches, but also on plays that he liked. In addition to leadership lessons, he devoted pages to offensive sets and defensive philosophies. Kerr began writing down plays that he liked and thought he could use someday while he watched games on TV at his San Diego home. When he saw something he liked, he would pause the TV to get a better feel for the play. Then he contacted his friend Kelly Peters, a coach at nearby Torrey Pines High at the time, to ask him to put the footage in a usable format. Peters, now a Warriors advance scout, placed the footage into iMovie for Kerr to study. The file, called ATOs for After Timeout, grew each passing week.

Ballard writes, "By the spring of 2014, the video library had swelled to over 50 plays and the Word file had morphed into a detailed Powerpoint presentation."

He didn't stop at plays. Ballard noted that Kerr also included details on "everything from a policy for families traveling on the road to whether players are required to do 20 minutes of cardio after a game if they don't play a certain number of minutes."

All of this preparation clearly helped Kerr hit the ground running. There was no need for him to spend a year learning the ropes, since he's already spent years preparing for his opportunity. So when he did get a chance with the Golden State Warriors, he was able to use that knowledge to win an NBA championship his first year.

Review Questions:

1. Who are you surrounding yourself with? Are you learning from them? Whether it's your coaches, your friends, or other mentors that you are able to find, what are you learning from them? Are you analyzing why your current boss is in the position that they are in? What does your supervisor do that is so effective? What do they do that is ineffective? Drill down and really analyze the performers around you.

2. How much extra work are you putting into learning about your craft? Do you take the extra time to learn things outside of your current responsibilities? Are you learning about the issues that you will need to know in your next position?

Steve Kerr was working as a television analyst, yet was using that time to learn about coaching. So if you are currently a vice-president, and want to be president, be sure to study the issues that the president would face. If you are currently an assistant coach, think about the topics that a head coach would face and develop your own philosophy.

3. What are you doing to prepare yourself for the dream job? If you had an interview tomorrow for a top CEO position, or head coach position, would you be prepared? Would you be able to list down all of the plays you would run, or how you would create a team culture? Would you be able to list what types of players you would want to have, and how you would structure the daily activities?

When Steve Kerr interviewed for the head coaching job, he already had his coaching philosophy fully developed. He had years of notes and an entire video file of plays that he liked and wanted to use.

Part Two: Building a Team Culture

Core Values

Any great team or organization must start with a basic set of values. Whether it's expressed through the mission statement, as a guiding set of principles, or simply in the day-to-day operations, every great organization must have something that all members follow and agree upon.

When dealing with an organization with high-performing individuals such as an NBA team, getting everyone to follow a set of values may be difficult. Each player has their own ego, their own strengths, and their own beliefs about their skill level. One of the top priorities of any leader is to get everyone to buy into a set of core values.

"By human nature, we're all selfish and we we want what's best for us," Kerr was quoted by Don Yaeger in Forbes. "In sports, this often translate into points, notoriety, and shots-per-game."

According to Kerr, the role of the head coach is to get these players to go against their natural instincts of being selfish and to find a way to get everyone to come together as a team.

"To get a group of highly competitive people to play roles and sacrifice for the team for the greater good is really hard, which is why it isn't often done very often," Kerr says. "In order to accomplish this, principles and details must be stressed in practice every day, even when against best interests of the individual. We are here for a reason, and there should be no compromise."

Kerr understands that simply telling his players to come together as a team is not enough. Human beings have a range of complex emotions, so simply telling them to "play for the team" is not enough. Kerr believes that a set of core values and principles must be shared and followed every day in order for the team to come together.

Assistant Coach Luke Walton (to be the head coach of the Los Angeles Lakers starting in the 2016-2017 season) explained to Tim Kawakami of the San Jose Mercury News what those values are.

"The first one and the most important one is probably joy–he wants us having **fun**," Walton said of the values that Kerr pushes to the team. "It's a long season, this game's meant to be fun."

"There's **mindfulness**," Walton continued, which he elaborated to mean that players should not get caught up in chasing their individual stats but to be "mindful of the right way to do things."

"There's **compassion** – for each other and for the game of basketball."

"And then there's **competition**. When we hit those four things, we're not only very tough to beat, but we're very fun to watch, we're very fun to coach, we're very fun to be around."

The Warriors have become fun to watch and tough to beat because Steve Kerr has been able to create the ultimate team culture with his players. Zach Lowe, NBA writer for ESPN, previously wrote in Grantland about a single play that clearly showed how the team has bought into what Kerr was preaching.

The play was a simple basket that took place over the course of a long season. Draymond Green, the Warriors forward, passed up an open 3 to make an extra pass to Marreese Speights. The extra pass didn't change the course of the game, as it took place in the final minute of the first quarter. But as Lowe explained, that extra pass by Green was clear proof that this team loves playing with each other.

When Lowe later asked Green about the play, Draymond responded: "I know exactly what play you're talking about." According to Green, "The guys on this team just know how to get each other going." For example, Draymond likes to make some defensive stops to get in the groove. Some players, like Marreese

Speights, like to make a couple of shots to get into a rhythm for the rest of the game. "Nothing wrong with that. That's just who he is," Green said of Speights. "And I know that. So that pass - that's what you do. That's what we do."

"It's such a selfless play," Lowe writes. "It is tangible basketball generosity, and every Golden State game has a half-dozen instances of such above-and-beyond sharing. All that giving has to add up to something. The knowledge that every teammate truly wants the best for you, and will sacrifice whatever it takes in the moment to help both you and the team - that has to be a powerful feeling. It must will you to do special things in return, and when everyone has that will inside of them, true team greatness can grow."

This philosophy of team play isn't a concept that exists simply because it sounds good. This isn't a touchy-feely type of issue where selflessness
 is preached because it is a noble cause. The Warriors preach team first because it gets results and is a huge competitive advantage over the rest of the league.

As Lowe writes, "The Warriors play liquid basketball." The team culture and philosophy that Steve Kerr has built with the Warriors "make you believe in the larger spiritual underpinnings of team sports. They are so in tune with each other, and that synchronization guides them on both ends of the floor." Their team culture creates a team that is able to seamlessly switch on defense when guarding players. It allows them to tire out opposing teams because they are always moving the ball to find the best shot. And it allowed them to win an NBA championship and then set the record for most wins in an NBA regular season the following year.

Adjust Your Strategy To Your Players

Once a set of core values is in place, Kerr then starts the process of building upon that foundation. When building up the new culture, Kerr still remains flexible to adjust to the individual needs and personalities of all of his players. Kerr understands that each player can work together for the greater good of the team but still maintain their uniqueness.

This lesson was something that Steve Kerr learned while playing for the San Antonio Spurs. As Kerr told Scott Cacciola of the New York Times, Argentinian star Manu Ginobili was in his first season with the Spurs and would often drive Head Coach Gregg Popovich up the wall with his circus passes. Eventually, after one too many turnovers, Popovich turned to Ginobili and asked him why he felt it was so necessary to do those high-risk passes.

"Pop, this is what I do."

That answer was apparently enough for Popovich, as he "gradually came to accept Manu being Manu as part of the package," writes Cacciola.

Kerr has carried that lesson with him to the Warriors, as he coaches a once-in-a-lifetime player like Stephen Curry. "There's a certain amount of that on this team because of the skill involved, especially with Steph," Kerr said. "Steph's going to throw some of the around-the-back stuff. He's going to make some crazy plays. And obviously so much more of it is good than bad, so you live with it."

Whether it's allowing Curry to shoot a three from 33 feet out to allowing Draymond Green to express his emotions on the court, Kerr believes that he can give his players the room to be themselves while still maintaining a successful organization. Too often, leaders believe that they must rule over their program and remove any sort of individual personality. What Kerr does instead is focus in on the key areas that he believes are important and lets the players be themselves in other areas.

Bruce Fraser, an Assistant Coach on the Warriors, explains that Kerr knows that the players like Curry want to express themselves when they play. Like Pop with Ginobili, Kerr understands that Steph Curry likes to play a little loose. Rather than attempt to control Curry, Kerr allows him to play the way that he wants to, but remains absolutely firm on one key statistic: turnovers.

"Steph will sometimes ask me during a game, 'How many turnovers do I have?'", Fraser told the New York Times. "Because he knows that's a thing Steve doesn't like. He'll never ask about his shooting numbers during a game, or any other kind of stats. But the only thing he knows is that Steve harps on turnovers, so it's definitely on his mind."

Draymond Green, the runner-up for the Defensive Player of the Year for two years in a row, also appreciates Kerr allowing his players to be themselves. "Earlier this season I yelled at him during the game and he yelled back," Green told Chris Ballard. "Afterward I walked over to the sideline and said, 'My bad.' He said, 'Nah, you're fine. I love your passion, why would I try to stop that? That makes you the player who you are.'"

Use What Works

When Kerr took over as Warriors head coach, he replaced popular former player Mark Jackson. Prior to Jackson becoming head coach, the Warriors failed to reach the playoffs for 17 years. In his three seasons as head coach, Jackson had a 121-109 record and made it to the playoffs in two of the three seasons.

Despite the success of Jackson, the ownership group of the Warriors felt that a change was necessary. Majority owner Joe Lacob made his fortune in Silicon Valley, and explained the decision to make a head coaching change as a natural progression of a company that is growing.

"There's a different CEO that may be required to achieve success at different stages of an organization's development," Lacob told ESPN. "When you're a startup company it's one thing, when you're a small-growth company it's one thing and when you're a mature company that's trying to reach a billion in sales - or in this case win an NBA championship - perhaps that's a different person. And we just felt overall that we needed a different person."

So when Kerr took over the head coaching duties, there were many aspects in place that were clearly working, such as their tough, defensive mindset. Rather than let his ego take over, Kerr understood that a solid foundation was already built. After all, the team was coming off a 51-win season. He didn't feel the need to start from scratch, and instead took the approach to use what had been working. He took his time, observing the team to figure out where improvement was needed.

In an article for NBA.com, Shaun Powell discusses how Kerr didn't allow his ego to get in the way after he took over the team, and how he manages the team. "Kerr wasn't bent on trying to prove himself different than Jackson. He's not claiming to have all the answers. He doesn't call many timeouts and once in the huddle rarely dwells on mistakes."

"The key thing I wanted to do was keep doing what they've done and how good they've been," said Kerr. "I didn't want to be the know-it-all-guy who came in and said, 'We've got to change this, we've got to change that.' This thing was already building and the foundation was already set."

Kerr mentioned to Powell that a big part of it was showing respect to the players. By respecting his players and what they previously accomplished, Kerr was able to come in create a cohesive team. These players have already worked for years to get to where they are today; they want to get better, but they want someone to come alongside them to show them what is working rather than institute system-wide changes. Kerr understood that if he pushed for too many changes in a system that was already successful, he would get push-back.

"My whole approach coming in was, 'Let's take what you have already done and let's try to keep it moving forward; let's try to get better'," Kerr told Sam Smith of NBA.com. "You can't come in and be a know it all. You've got to come in and respect what guys have done individually and as a team and find out how can we get better. We have great guys, all very receptive. I found out they were incredibly coachable and willing listeners and good guys. You could feel right away this was a team that would have good chemistry."

The way that Kerr approached his players clearly worked. In his first two years as head coach, superstar Stephen Curry has won the NBA's MVP award. When Curry was accepting his first MVP award, he stated that Kerr's ability to come in to the team and guide it without having a large ego clearly helped him and the team.

"You're very humble in the way you've approached the season," Curry said. "You're a huge reason why we're here today. Thank you for being you."

Good Ideas Can Come From Anywhere

Kerr's ability to control his own ego allows him to listen to others. He knows that he doesn't have all of the answers, and is willing to let his staff contribute meaningful ideas. This key trait was one of the key reason that Kerr was able to guide the team during the NBA Finals in 2015.

After winning the first game of the Finals, the Warriors lost the next two games. Lebron James and the bigger Cavaliers were using the size and strength to slow down the game and play a physically demanding style of basketball. The Warriors clearly needed to do something to change up the series, or they risked being physically beaten.

Enter Nick U'Ren.

U'Ren isn't technically a coach or a scout on the Warriors. His title was Special Assistant to the Head Coach. Kerr first met U'Ren when Kerr was the General Manager for the Phoenix Suns, and U'Ren was the assistant video coordinator. "The idea is that rather than have a 45-year old woman behind a desk answering mail as your assistant, why not instead use that spot to add another young basketball mind to the staff," Kerr said of the decision to bring on U'Ren to the Warriors.

As far as U'Ren knows, he's the only person in the NBA who has his jobs. And what exactly are his responsibilities? Here is how Lee Jenkins explained some of his duties:

"He compiles the playlist that the Warriors blare during practice, alternating between Aerosmith and Drake. He edits the videos that they show during film sessions, splicing Klay Thompson highlights with Draymond Green spoofs. He rebounds for Stephen Curry, adding up his made three-pointers from every spot. When Steve Kerr has a radio interview, U'Ren is the one who reminds him, and when Kerr stages a bowling tournament, U'Ren is the one who divides the teams."

However, due to the work culture that Kerr created, this 28 year old was empowered enough to make a coaching suggestion that quite possibly changed the entire series.

On the night after falling behind the Cavs 2 games to 1, U'Ren pulled up video from the previous NBA Finals. In the 2014 Finals, the San Antonio Spurs faced the Miami Heat. With the series being tied at one game apiece, Spurs Head Coach Gregg Popovich made a starting lineup change, pulling out Tiago Splitter for the much smaller Boris Diaw. After the lineup change, the Spurs blew out the Heat to win the NBA championship.

Nick U'Ren thought that the Warriors could do the same to the Cavaliers. He came up with an idea to substitute center Andrew Bogut with the small forward Andre Iguodala. The move would be a big decision, as Bogut started in 65 games that year while Iguodala started in none. However, he brought up the idea with Assistant Coach Luke Walton that night, and worked out how the move might free up space for the smaller Warriors to play at a faster pace. Walton agreed.

At 3:00 am, U'Ren sent out a text to Steve Kerr with his idea. The next morning, the Warriors staff met at the Ritz Carlton in Cleveland and discussed the merits of the idea. If they chose to make the lineup change, the decision would have huge implications. The Warriors won 67 games that year with Andrew Bogut starting. Now, suddenly, in the middle of the NBA Finals, they were changing their starting lineup. If they lost Game 4, then the Cavs would be one win away from winning the title. Questions of Kerr's competence and whether he could handle the high-level decision making of an NBA Finals would take over sports media. It would be understandable if a coach decided to keep his lineup in place. After all, it got them that far.

Yet, Kerr decided to make the change. Iguodala started in Game 4, and the impact was immediate. The Warriors won the game 103-82, with Iguodala holding Lebron James to 20 points. Iguodala himself outscored James with 22 points. The lineup change worked out so well that Andre Iguodala was named NBA Finals MVP, as the Warriors didn't lose another game in the Finals.

"It was his decision," Luke Walton told Sports Illustrated about the lineup change made by Kerr. "It's always his decision. But this is why he's the greatest boss in the world. We can all make suggestions, even a video guy, and he'll seriously consider them".

"I was never that nervous," Nick U'Ren said to Yahoo Sports about the idea. "Our staff is so amazing that they would never throw anyone under the bus or hang them out to dry. And obviously, they are being super kind for giving me credit. I was definitely happy when it worked because I wanted to win."

U'Ren continues, "Steve deserves all of the credit because he has to live and die with the consequences. It's easy to make a suggestion, but he has to make a decision."

Kerr, in his typical low-key demeanor, said that he decision wasn't that risky. As he told Yahoo Sports, "I don't think it was that gutsy because they were kicking our ass."

Review Questions:

1. What are the core values of your organization? What does it stand for? What are the values that are passed on to the members of the organization? And more importantly, are they listening? If we selected two people in your organization at random and asked them what the values are, would they both tell us the same thing?

2. Are your ideas on how to run the organization in alignment with the type of people your organization has? Are you attempting to force your players to fit into your system, when your system is meant for different types of players? Did you modify your plans or strategy to line up with the type of resources you have? Or are you ignoring reality and trying to force your players and resources into something that it's not?

3. Does everyone in the organization feel as if their voices are being heard? Regardless of position or title, can someone offer up their suggestions on improvement to the boss? Are you willing to listen to those ideas?

Part Three: Mindset

Aside from the ways in which Steve Kerr builds his team, another interesting aspect of Kerr is his coaching philosophy. As the child of academics, Steve Kerr has a very unique perspective on the world, which has clearly contributed to his success. In this section, we'll cover the mindset of Steve Kerr and how he applies that to his coaching.

Empathy

The ability to get 12 Alpha Males on an NBA team to work together towards a common goal is not an easy task. By default, every single player on an NBA locker room was the best player on their team in high school and college. The worst player on an NBA team is still in the top half percent of basketball players in the entire world. The job of a head coach tasked with controlling their egos, keeping their confidence up, and getting them to work together can be fraught with difficulties.

So how does he do it? How does Steve Kerr make sure that everyone on the team is on the same page, and that everyone understands their role on the team?

The first idea that Steve Kerr uses to manage his team is to understand the needs of every single player. With the reigning NBA MVP on his team, Kerr could very well just spend all of his time and attention on Stephen Curry. He could treat Curry like the superstar that he is, and cater to every one of his needs. He could do this and probably still make the playoffs each year.

But to Kerr, keeping every player engaged is one of the keys to team success. As Chris Ballard of Sports Illustrated wrote, "Kerr strives to mimic Phil Jackson, who 'never let anybody rot at the end of the bench.'"

"In ways, the guys at the end of the bench define your chemistry," Kerr says. "And if you ignore them, and they never play, they're going to get bitter. And all of the sudden it becomes insidious."

In a discussion with Shaun Powell of NBA.com, Kerr acknowledges that his past on the bench and influenced the way he now manages his players.

"I relate best to bench guys, because I was one," Kerr said. "Coaching is about managing guys at the bottom of the rotation more than the starters. You've got to have compassion. You've got to keep them engaged."

The way that Kerr manages to keep all of his players engaged is to simply communicate with them. "Take a guy like (backup center) Mo Speights," Center Andrew Bogut told Powell. "He's hit some game-winning shots for us and then had games when he didn't even play, but Steve's kept him abreast the whole time. Sometimes when he keeps players on the bench too long, he'll apologize to them. I think that's important. He's not afraid to admit if he believes he made a mistake. You can say something to him, something you may not like about what we're doing or how you're being used, and he doesn't take anything personally."

Bogut acknowledges that Kerr has earned the respect of his players by treating them all equally, regardless of status, and asking for input from them: "Every couple of weeks he'll meet with guys individually and get their thoughts about how they're playing and what they need to do to get better and what he needs to do," said Bogut. "It's open dialogue. There's no agendas, nothing personal, no favorites."

After taking the head coaching position, Kerr surprised players by coming to meet them in the off-season to discuss strategy. Instead of simply calling Curry and leaving the other men out of it, Kerr sought to speak to all of his key players in face-to-face meetings. This approach led to players who appreciated Kerr's strategy and acceptance of his position at head coach. According to Ballard, "Over the weeks that followed, Kerr met with a number of other players, including flying to Australia to see Bogut. He gave them all the same message. Here is what I'm hoping to do, here's why and here's how. The players, some of whom had been conspicuously silent when Kerr got hired, appreciated the no-BS approach."

Have Fun

The ability to connect with his players, to emphasize with their struggles, and to understand what it is that they are going through is one of Kerr's greatest strength. The simple fact of the matter is that Kerr understands that any team, organization, or group is made up of people. They all may have different strengths and weaknesses, but in the end, they are all people who want to be a part of something meaningful, and have fun while doing it.

One key aspect of his coaching philosophy when he took over the Warriors was to make sure that his players were happy. In Sports Illustrated, Chris Ballard stated that among Kerr's belief "was that this is a players' league, and players need to be happy. And when you spend roughly two-thirds of the year together, seven days a week, sometimes your greatest opponent is monotony."

The NBA season is a long grind. The season opens in November, and teams playing deep into the playoffs can see their season end in May or June. Each team must travel to 41 away games during the year, with some games being on back to back nights. It is very easy for the players to simply get bogged down.
To battle against sluggishness, Chris Ballard writes that Kerr creates a practice environment that is "based around a simple concept: Athletes are more productive, and happier, when they're not bored."

He accomplishes this through several ways. Some are simple. For example, as previously mentioned, Kerr has no problem learning from others and using their techniques if it works. So when Kerr met Seattle Seahawks Head Football Coach Pete Carroll and learned that Carroll likes to blast music during practice, Kerr quickly turned on the speakers at the Warriors practice facility.

Kerr also likes to break up the day to day activities of his staff as well. Lee Jenkins wrote about one such instance in Sports Illustrated when Kerr suddenly stopped a staff meeting and told all of his assistants to climb into Luke Walton's SUV. "They drove 30 miles to Muir Beach, stripped down to their boxers and jumped into the bracing Pacific," writes Jenkins.

"'Do s___ or go have fun', player development coach Bruce Fraser cracked that day, a throwaway line that has become an organizational mantra."

Maintain Perspective

Kerr believes that having fun as a team largely contributes to the team's success and helps the players maintain perspective. In an interview with Marc J. Spears of *Yahoo! Sports*, Kerr discussed the need to keep his players happy.

"In the end, it's still the title that matters the most," Kerr said. "Having said that, this team, one of the reasons they are special is they take so much joy in the process of each game. They don't talk much about records. But our guys have a lot of fun from one night to the next. I think that's part of our success. It comes from enjoying everything every day."

Kerr discussed his perspective on the game with Jenkins. He does not fit the typical prototype of a coach. He has plenty of hobbies that do not involve the game of basketball but still contribute to his ability to see the game through a wider lens. He realizes how fortunate he and the players are to make a living doing something they love. This perspective is not often found in the world of professional sports, but Kerr manages to maintain his perspective by focusing on activities outside of basketball while realizing the value of his team.

"We make a living in basketball. This is unbelievable. This is a joke. How did this happen? It's good to think about that. It's important for our players to think about it. **You have to separate the seriousness of your craft, working to achieve something special, while recognizing the absurdity of it all.**"

This is something that many high achieving individuals fail to remember. It is possible to take your craft seriously and still understand that it's just one part of your life. The two thoughts can exist at the same time. A person can be dedicated to their sport, their coaching career, their job, and do it to the best of the ability. But they can **ALSO** appreciate their overall life. They can still enjoy their family and friends. They can still have interests or enjoyment that does not involve the craft. Spending time with loved ones does not mean a person is not dedicated to their job. Enjoying mystery books or watching foreign movies on the weekends does not mean a lack of dedication to their craft.

In fact, Steve Kerr believes that keeping things in perspective and having interests outside of basketball helps his team achieve their success. One way that Kerr does this is to invite guest presenters to practice as part of an effort to encourage the Warriors players to see the world outside of basketball. Michael Lewis, author of *Moneyball*, *The Big Short*, and *The Blind Side*, spoke to the team about success and the value of perspective. Lewis told the team that success led to fewer people who were willing to be honest with him. They were not willing to tell him when his work wasn't good enough. Stephen Curry was especially impacted by Lewis' message and shared his thoughts with reporters after practice.

"He said the more he became successful, the less people wanted to tell him that," Curry said. "So he really cherished the couple voices he had around him that would keep it straight with him, no matter how big his name got, no matter how many awards he won, no matter how many best sellers he had. He had one editor in particular, but always a couple voices he can rely on to shoot him straight, which is great advice for anybody in our profession."

One of the things that makes Kerr so successful at maintaining his perspective is his ability to find things to enjoy outside the game of basketball. Kerr is an avid, eclectic reader, a skill he learned from his father. He constantly studies a variety of topics that have nothing to do with the world of basketball, but that he can apply when he is coaching and interacting with players or the media. He works to pass on this ability to remove himself from the game to his players.

Ilan Mochari of INC.com examines Kerr's love of reading, which includes topics far removed from sports. Reading provides Kerr time to be alone and allows his thoughts to wander. His ability to incorporate the lessons learned from outside the game is evident in the success that he has had with the Warriors. Mochari writes, "you won't find basketball or even sports books on his night stand. So far this year, he has read articles about Al Pacino, Ronald Reagan's astrologer, wrongful incarceration, and musical duo Hall and Oates. Next on his list is an article about the man who plays Big Bird on 'Sesame Street.'"

Mochari wonders what this successful coach gains from such a diverse reading list, and Warriors general manager Bob Myers provided the answer in an interview with the Wall Street Journal: "He likes to remind the players that there's more to life than basketball. Whatever is going on with our team or his coaching staff is not the most important thing going on in the world."

Understanding What Truly Matters

Steve Kerr understands that there is more to life than just basketball. Born in Beirut to parents who were academics, Kerr spent a childhood growing up in international locales such as Cairo. "I developed a lot of compassion living in Egypt, seeing the poverty," Kerr told the San Jose Mercury News. "The discussions around the dinner table about world politics and understanding how fortunate we were - all that helped me gain perspective on life. That helped with teammates when I was a player and now as coach."

The reason for Kerr's international upbringing was due to the career of his father, Malcolm Kerr. The senior Kerr was an expert in Middle East politics, and was serving as the President of American University in Beirut. Malcolm was dedicating his life to bringing the Western world and the Middle East together.

However, as Ian O'Connor writes in a moving article in ESPN, that life was tragically cut short on Jan. 18, 1984, "when two Islamic terrorists ambushed Malcolm outside his university office and shot him in the back of the head for the crime of being an American."

"Lebanon had descended into civil war, and an anti-Western fervor colored the chaos," O'Connor explains. "The 52-year old educator, peacemaker and author who dedicated his everything to improving relations between the U.S. and the Arab world was murdered in the same building where he had met his wife, Ann, in 1954, and was pronounced dead in the same hospital where he had been born."

Steve Kerr was a freshman living in the student-athletes dorms at the University of Arizona when he received the news. Not knowing how to process it, Kerr just started running around the streets of Tucson in the middle of the night.

The family and Steve decided that he should remain at Arizona instead of flying over to Beirut. The family was planning to have a memorial service for Malcolm at his alma mater Princeton, as well as at UCLA, where he was a teacher for over 20 years.

Two nights after his father's death, Steve was playing in a game for Lute Olson and the Arizona Wildcats. "Steve wept during a pregame moment of silence, came off the bench to his his first jumper - a 25-footer - and made 5 of 7 field goal attempts to give Olson his first Pac-10 victory," writes O'Connor.

As many who find themselves going through difficult times, Steve Kerr used the basketball court to find solace. "Steve used the basketball court as his sanctuary, his place to hide from the tragedy of losing the man who shot baskets with him in their Pacific Palisades driveway," O'Connor writes. "The man who would read The New Yorker in the Dodger Stadium bleachers while his young sons were trying to run down batting practice home runs. The man who would never see him play a college game in person."

Unfortunately, the harsh realities of the world would invade that sanctuary. In 1988, when Steve Kerr was starting as a fifth year senior, he was warming up before a game at rival Arizona State. As he took his warmup shots, a group of Arizona State "fans" thought that they would get under the skin of Kerr, and began directing some chants to him.

"P-L-O!"

"P-L-O!" (PLO stands for the Palestine Liberation Organization.)

"Where's your dad?!"

Radio host Tom Tolbert was Kerr's teammate at Arizona at the time. "I will never, ever forget that," he told Jon Wilner of the San Jose Mercury News. "It was the only time I've seen him break down."

Kerr sat down on the bench with tears in his eyes, trying to regain his composure. By the time that the opening tip came, Kerr was ready.

"He wasn't going to charge into the stands to go after those idiots," Kerr's younger brother Andrew tells O'Connor in ESPN. "He was just going to ruin their night by winning the game."

Kerr went on to make all six of his 3-point attempts in the first half. He ended the game with 22 points as the Wildcats blew out their rival.

"There's no question they made me play my best," Kerr said.

This incredibly difficult period of Steve Kerr's life has no doubt played an impact in his mindset. Although basketball is important to Steve, and he has been able achieve incredible success from it, he still fully understands that there are things in life that are more important than championships.

Steve's mom, Ann Curry, runs the Fulbright scholar program at UCLA. She told Ian O'Connor that to this day, there is still sadness over the death of her husband.

"My main regret, and the thing that brings the most pangs, is everything Malcolm missed," she told O'Connor in an interview. "The lives of his children, the fact that he never saw his grandchildren. That hurts tremendously."

As deep as the sadness was for the Kerr family, they have all been able to go on to achieve incredible success. Steve Kerr's oldest brother received an economics doctorate from Stanford, while his older sister got her doctorate in education from Harvard. Steve's younger brother worked for the National Security Council and later got his MBA. As Ann Kerr told Jon Wilner of the Mercury News, when referring to her children, she says "I have two Ph.Ds, one MBA, and one NBA."

When writing about Kerr, Ian O'Connor says something that can be applied to the entire family, and to all people who have been able to move past difficult times: That they are "a survivor scarred -- but not defined -- by tragedy."

Review Questions:

1. Do you understand that you can take your craft seriously and still have perspective? Do you understand that you can work hard, do your best, and commit yourself to your job but still have a life outside of it?

You can be dedicated at work, but still enjoy your family. You can be committed to practicing, but still enjoy a night out. Having interests outside of your craft does not mean you are not committed. It is possible to be both at the same time.

2. What do you do to break up boredom in your organization, or in your own routine? How do you keep your staff engaged in their work? How do you keep your players from going through the motions at practice?

Allowing your organization to enjoy practice or having a fun staff meeting does not mean that you are not dedicated to the job.

3. What is important to you besides your craft? Aside from winning a championship or closing a sale, what else is important in your life?

Conclusion

The job that Steve Kerr was able to accomplish is nothing short of remarkable. He took over from a popular head coach, got everyone on the team to buy into his new coaching style, and moved a former all-star to the bench without any drama. The results of his moves? An NBA Championship in his first year, and the best regular season record in NBA history for his second year.

What Kerr and the Warriors have been able to show us is that empathy, joy, and selflessness can play a key role in achieving success. By creating an environment where the leader understands the feelings of each individual, and where each individual feels empowered, Kerr was able to create one of the best teams in history of professional sports.

As Robert Silverman of The Daily Beast writes, this is one of the reason why everyone around the world loves to watch team sports achieve championships:

"Kerr was able to get a group of millionaire athletes, all of whom have been considered stars at one point in their amateur and pro careers, to sacrifice for the collective good because he made them feel that they were part of something great."

Steve Kerr's Keys to Success

1. Working to create a strong team not only makes the team better, it also make you better.

2. Learn all you can from the people who are you life.

3. Use all of the opportunities you have to seek out additional knowledge, even if it doesn't apply to your current responsibilities.

4. Create detailed plans about how you will tackle new jobs. Develop your management philosophy before you become a manager.

5. Every organization needs to have a set of core values.

6. Adjust to the resources and players you have. Use their skills and personalities to your advantage.

7. Good ideas can come from anywhere. Don't let your ego prevent you from getting advice or counsel from others.

8. Understand the feelings and motivation of everyone on your team by communicating with them.

9. Having fun activities and using humor to break up routine can help improve performance.

10. You can take your craft seriously and still maintain perspective in your life.

About Leadership Case Studies

Leadership Case Studies provides brief reports and analysis on successful individuals. We focus on the habits, strategies, and mindsets of high-performing people in the sports, business, and entertainment industries.

Links to the case studies articles, videos and speeches are all listed on the website.

Started in July 2015, Leadership Case Studies released its first case study on University of Alabama Football Coach Nick Saban, winner of 4 national championships.

Website:
http://www.leadershipcasestudies.com